THE PEANUTS
PIANO COLLECTION

© 2022 PEANUTS Worldwide LLC
www.snoopy.com

ISBN 978-1-70516-574-4

Visit Hal Leonard Online at
www.halleonard.com

World headquarters, contact:
Hal Leonard
7777 West Bluemound Road
Milwaukee, WI 53213
Email: info@halleonard.com

In Europe, contact:
Hal Leonard Europe Limited
42 Wigmore Street
Marylebone, London, W1U 2RN
Email: info@halleonardeurope.com

In Australia, contact:
Hal Leonard Australia Pty. Ltd.
4 Lentara Court
Cheltenham, Victoria, 3192 Australia
Email: info@halleonard.com.au

BON VOYAGE, CHARLIE BROWN

from BON VOYAGE, CHARLIE BROWN!

By VINCE GUARALDI

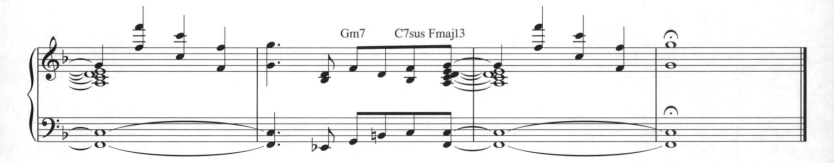

CHARLIE BROWN ALL STARS

from CHARLIE BROWN'S ALL STARS!

By VINCE GUARALDI

CHARLIE BROWN THEME

from A CHARLIE BROWN CHRISTMAS

By VINCE GUARALDI

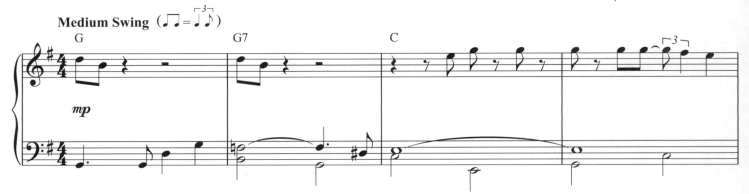

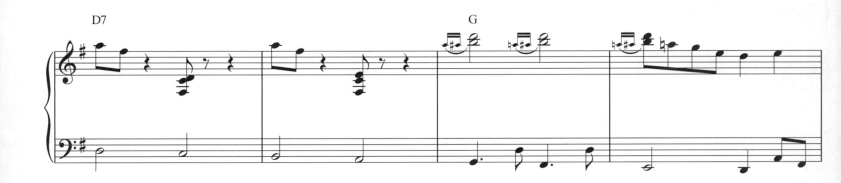

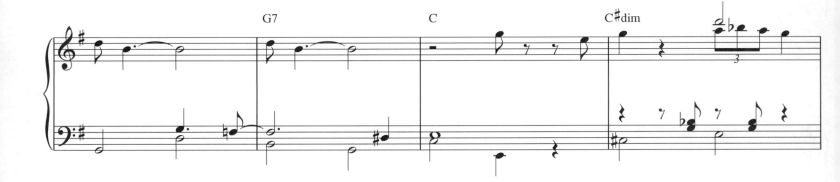

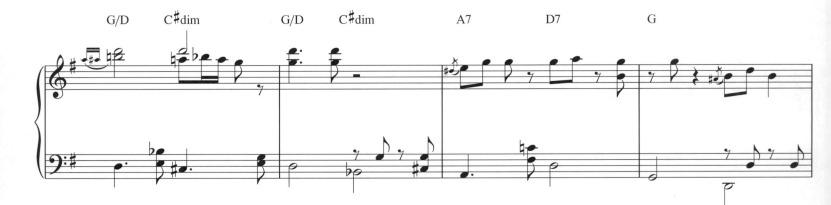

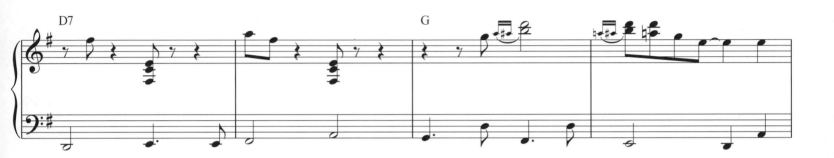

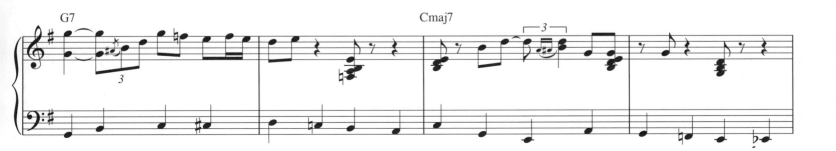

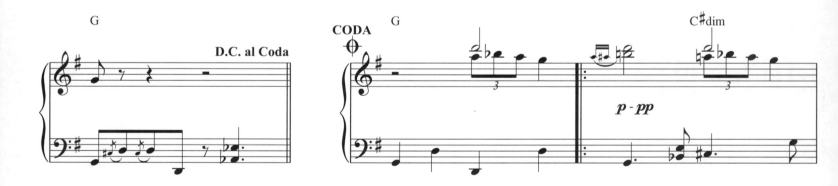

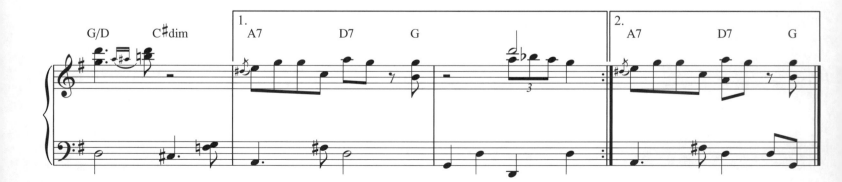

CHRISTMAS TIME IS HERE

from A CHARLIE BROWN CHRISTMAS

Words by LEE MENDELSON
Music by VINCE GUARALDI

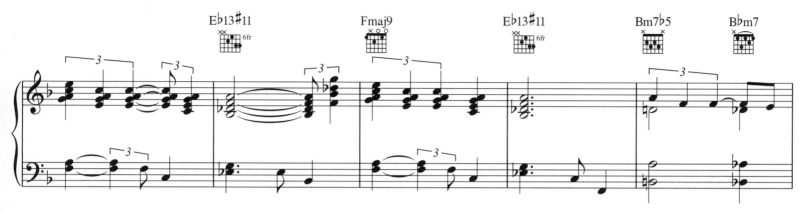

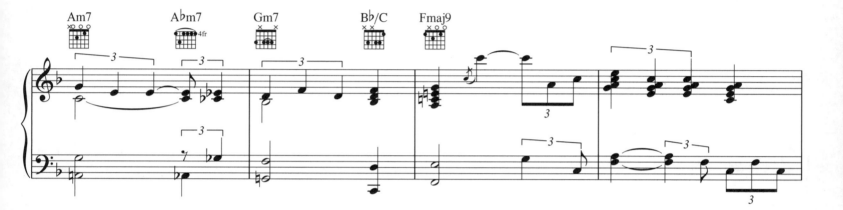

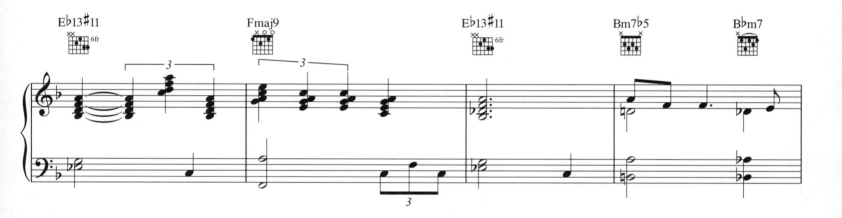

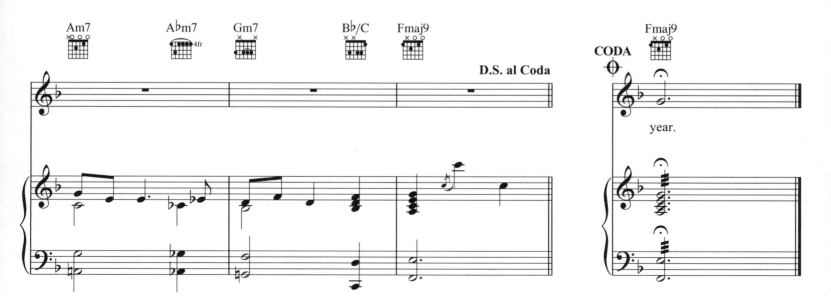

CHARLIE BROWN'S WAKE-UP

from BE MY VALENTINE, CHARLIE BROWN

By VINCE GUARALDI

Slowly, very expressively

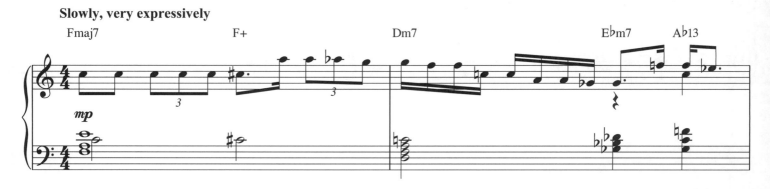

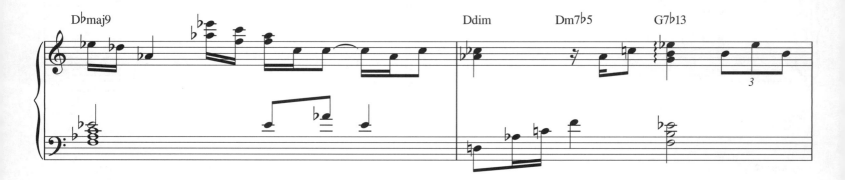

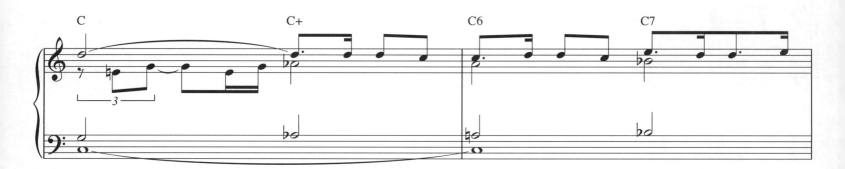

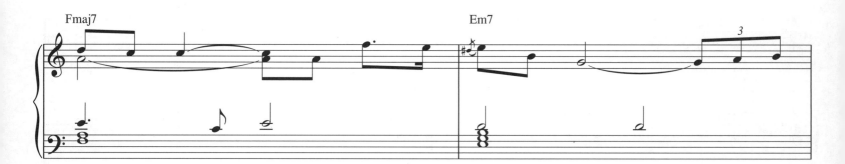

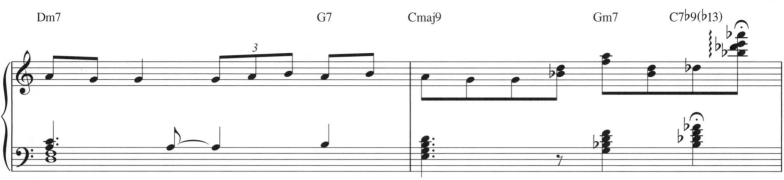

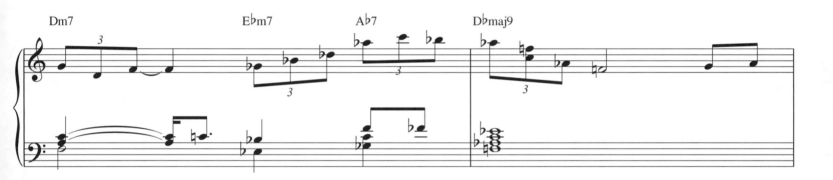

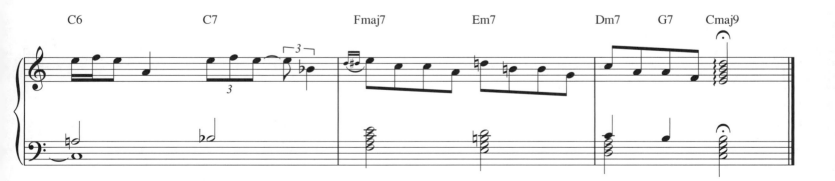

COPS AND ROBBERS
from IT'S A MYSTERY, CHARLIE BROWN

By VINCE GUARALDI

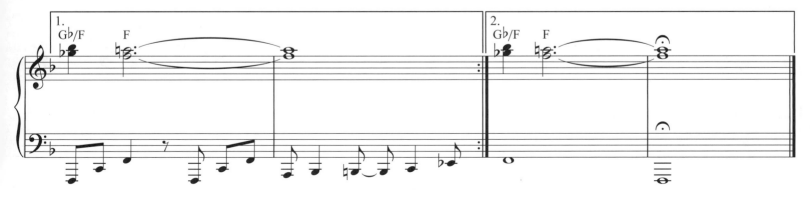

GRAVEYARD THEME
from IT'S THE GREAT PUMPKIN, CHARLIE BROWN

By VINCE GUARALDI

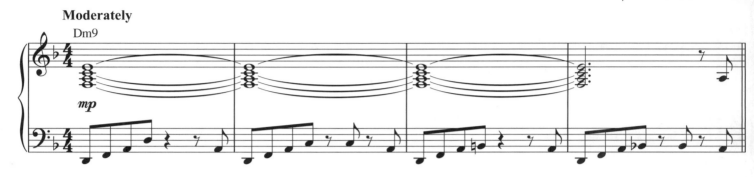

C13♯11
B13♯11
B♭13♯11
A13♯11
To Coda
Dm/A
A
Dm/A
A
Dm/A
A
F
G
Cm
Cm(maj7)
Cm7
Cm6
Cm

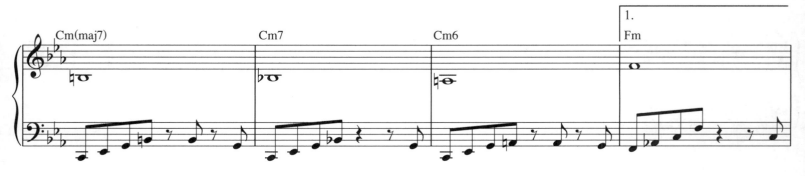

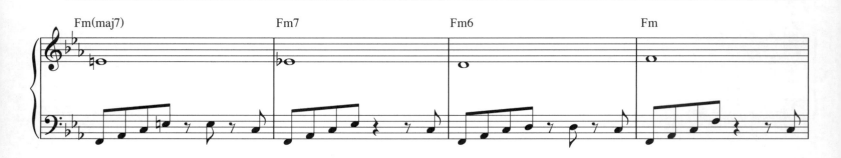

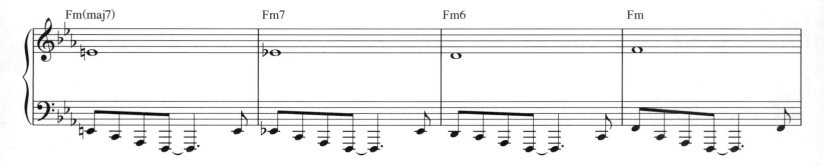

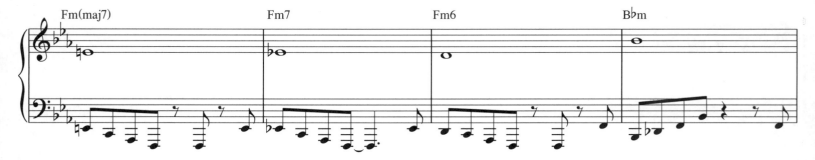

D.S. al Coda
(take repeats)

CODA

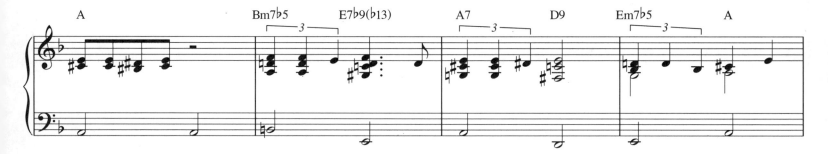

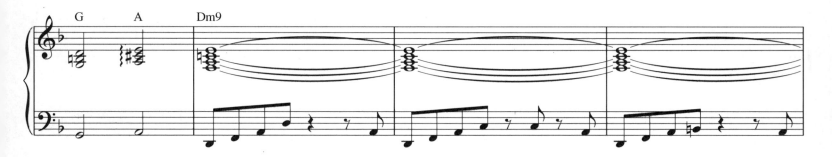

INCUMBENT WALTZ
from YOU'RE NOT ELECTED, CHARLIE BROWN

By VINCE GUARALDI

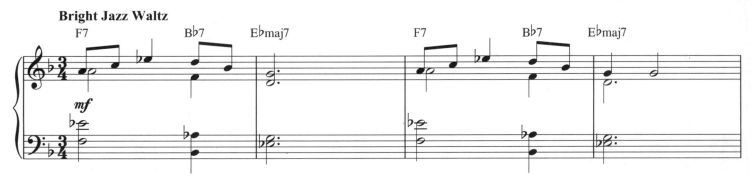

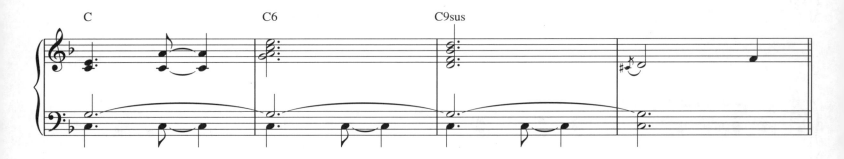

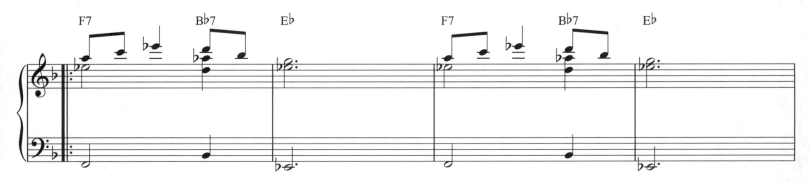

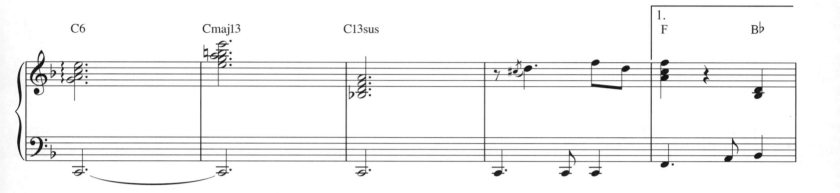

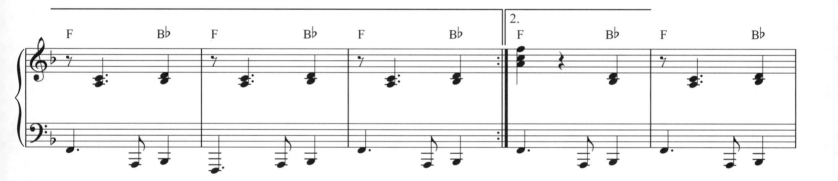

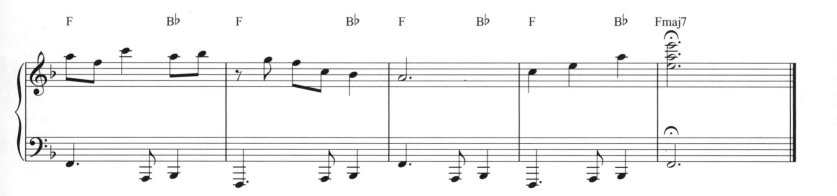

IT'S A MYSTERY, CHARLIE BROWN

from IT'S A MYSTERY, CHARLIE BROWN

By VINCE GUARALDI

Moderately fast

21

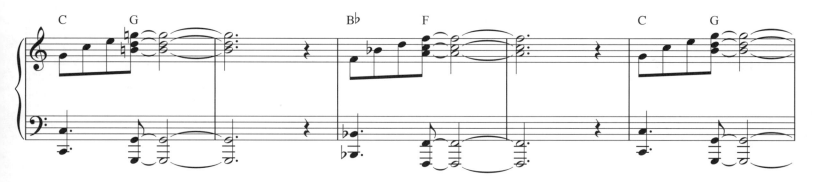

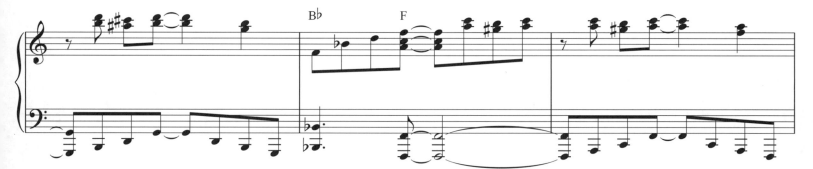

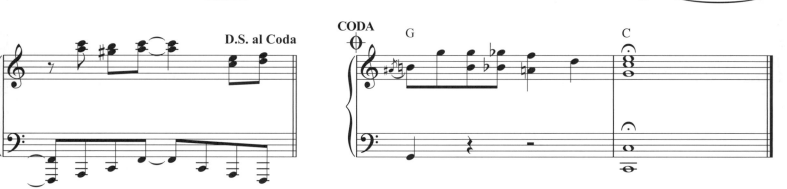

LINUS AND LUCY

from A CHARLIE BROWN CHRISTMAS

By VINCE GUARALDI

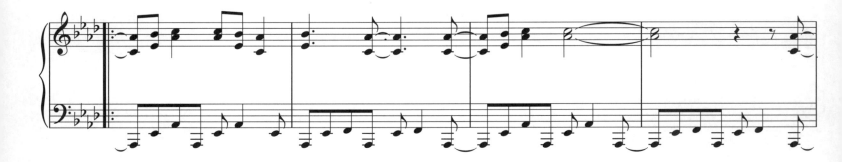

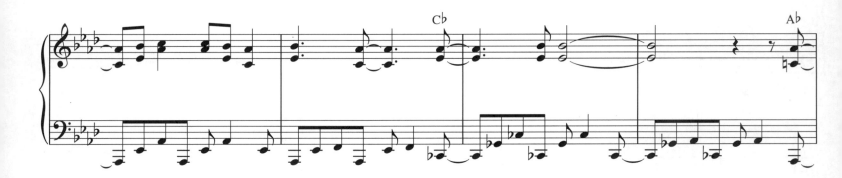

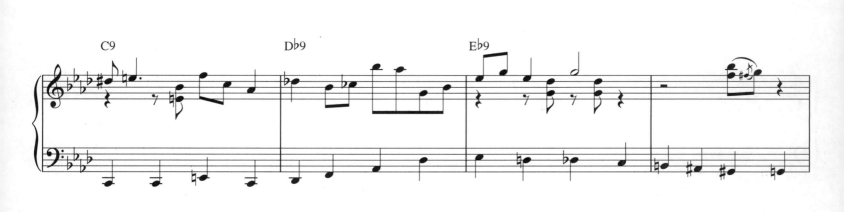

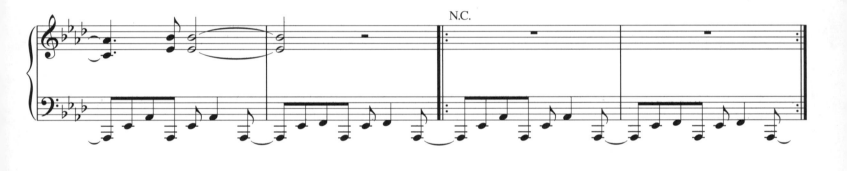

LITTLE RED-HAIRED GIRL

from YOU'RE IN LOVE, CHARLIE BROWN

By VINCE GUARALDI

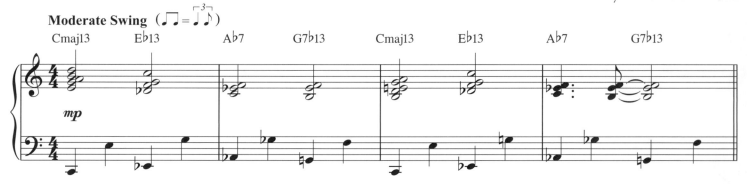

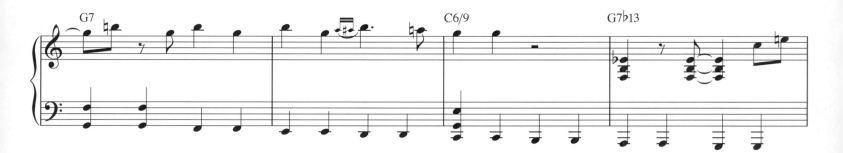

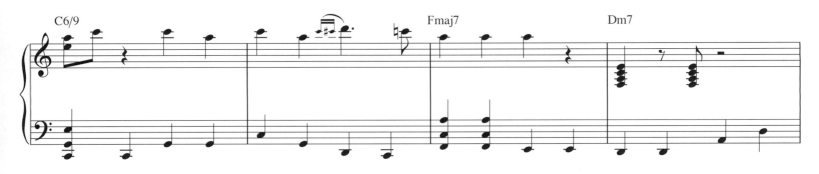

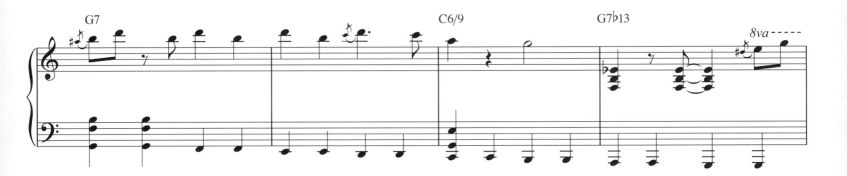

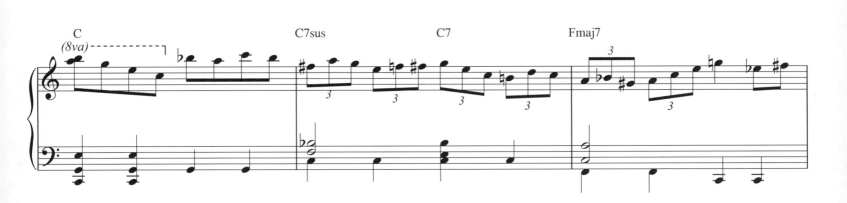

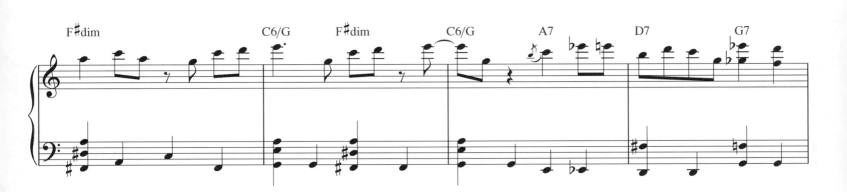

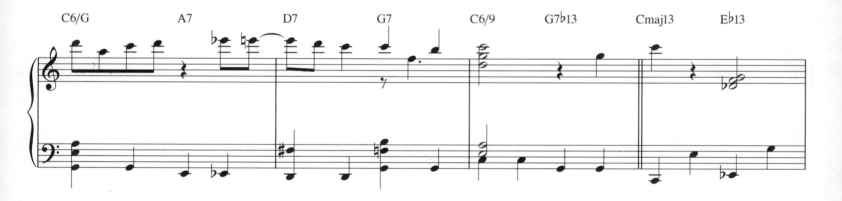

LOVE WILL COME
from YOU'RE IN LOVE, CHARLIE BROWN

By VINCE GUARALDI

Moderate Bossa

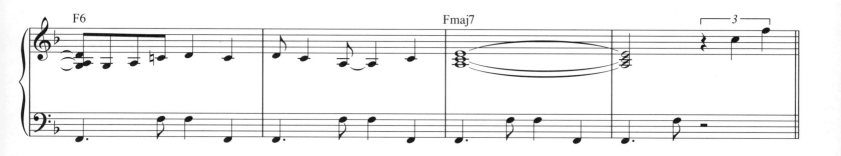

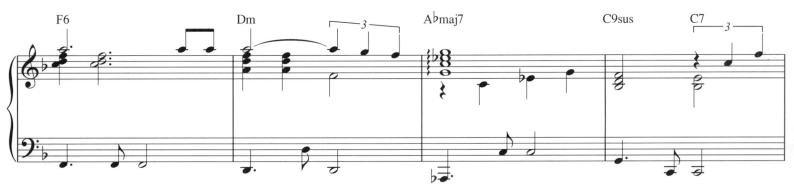

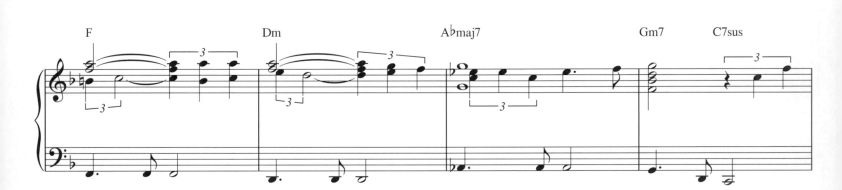

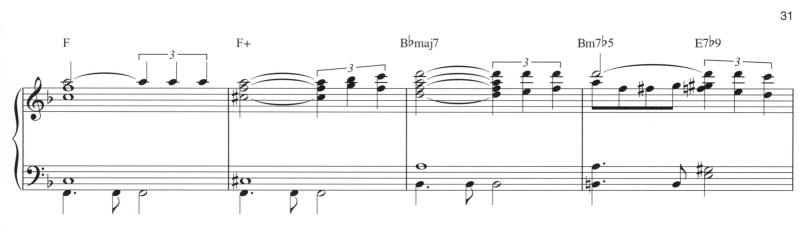

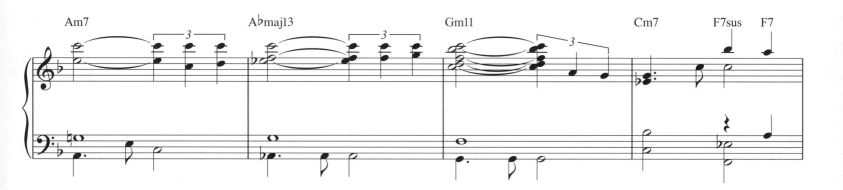

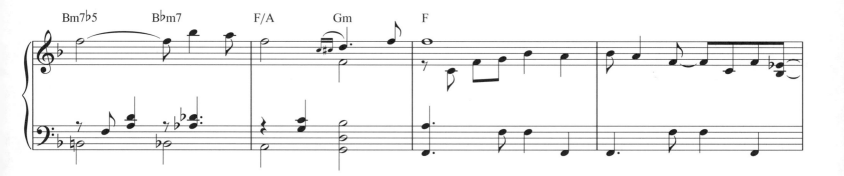

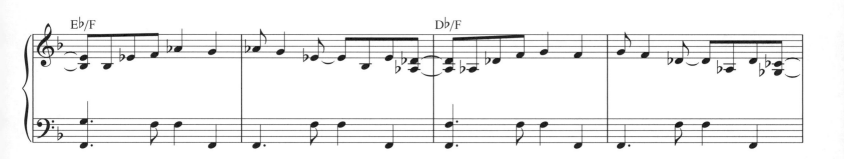

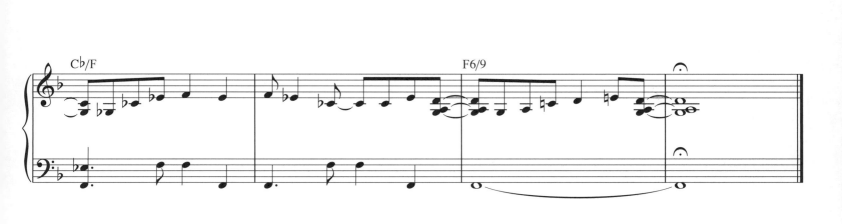

PAW PET OVERTURE
from BE MY VALENTINE, CHARLIE BROWN

By VINCE GUARALDI

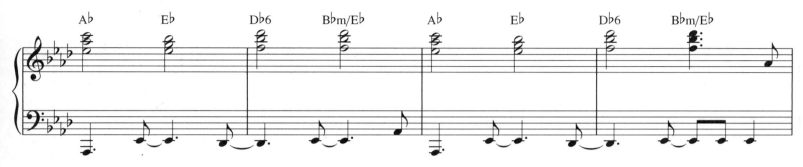

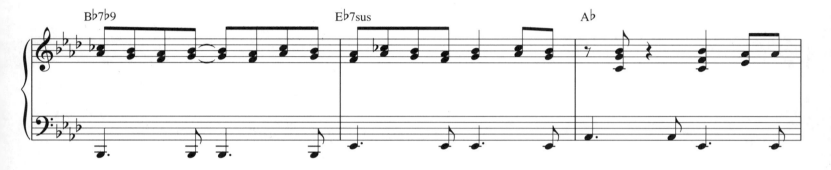

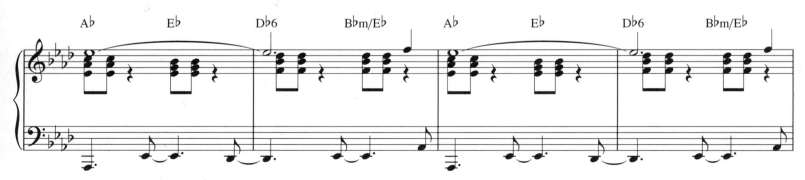

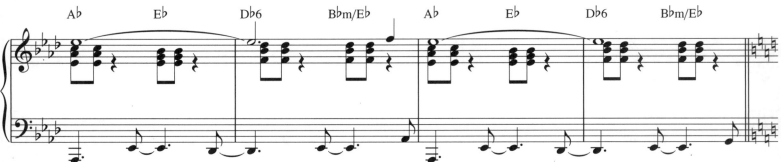

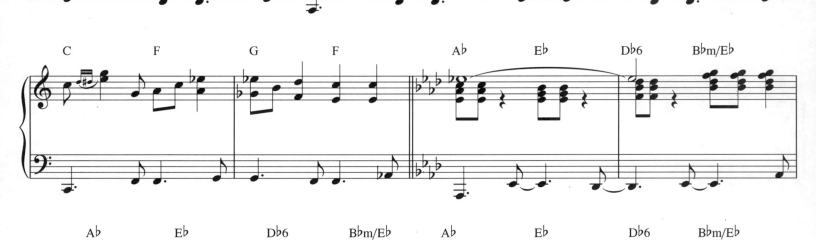

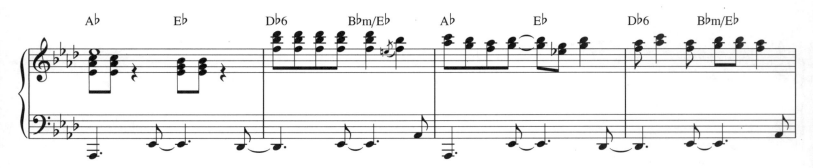

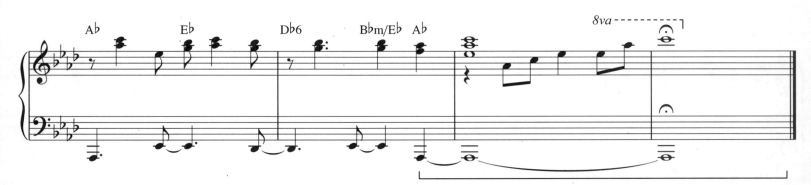

PITKIN COUNTY BLUES

from THERE'S NO TIME FOR LOVE, CHARLIE BROWN

By VINCE GUARALDI

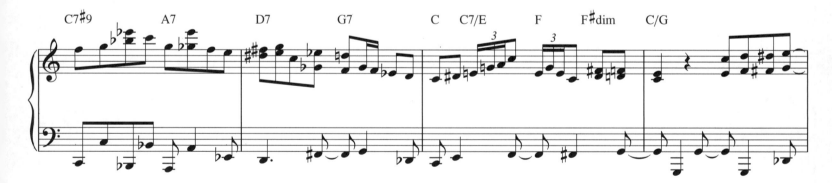

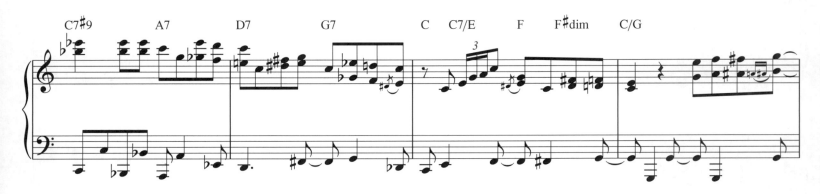

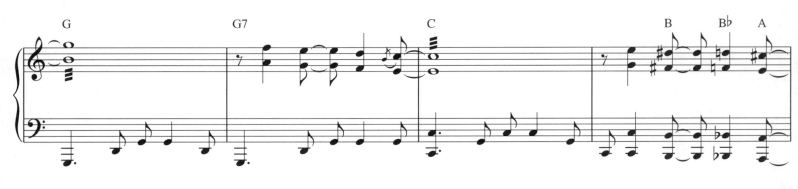

37

D.S. al Coda

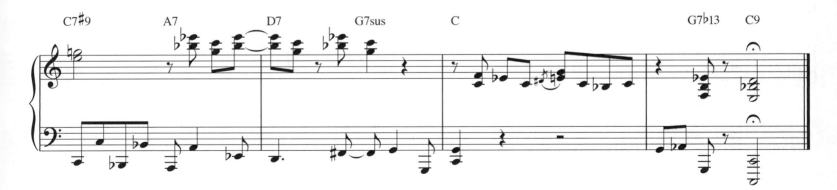

SASSY SALLY

from IT'S A MYSTERY, CHARLIE BROWN

By VINCE GUARALDI

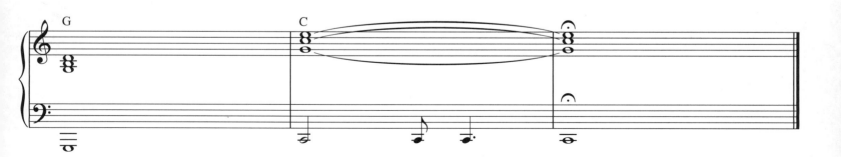

SCHOOL DAYS
from YOU'RE IN LOVE, CHARLIE BROWN

By WILL D. COBB
and GUS EDWARDS
Arranged by VINCE GUARALDI

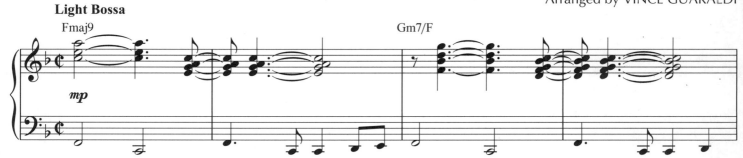

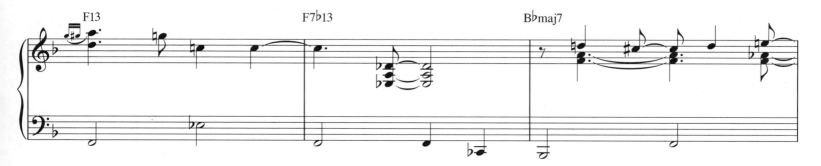

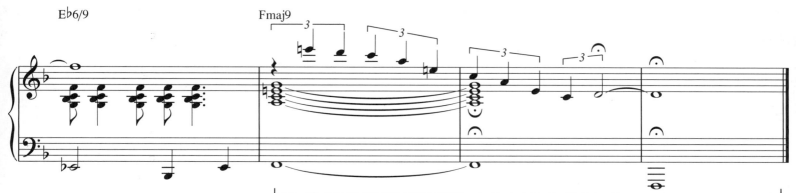

SCHROEDER'S WOLFGANG

from HE'S YOUR DOG, CHARLIE BROWN

By VINCE GUARALDI

Moderate Swing

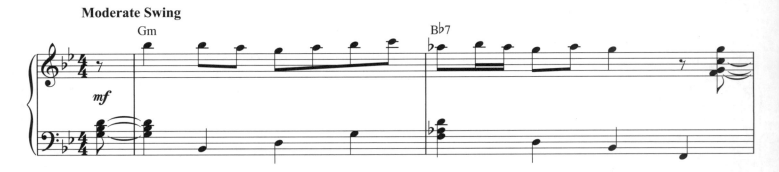

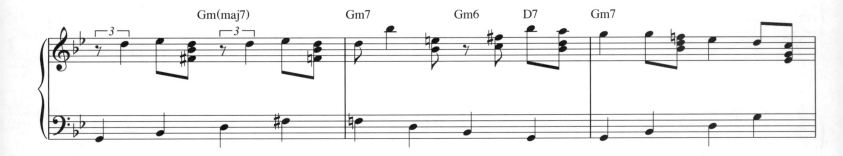

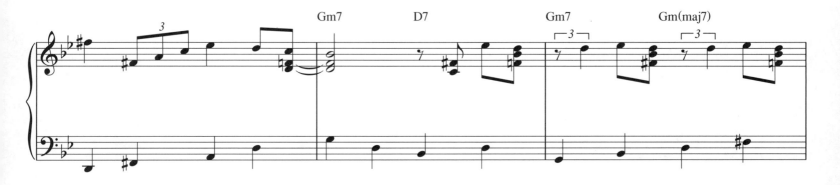

WOODSTOCK'S DREAM
from IT'S THE EASTER BEAGLE, CHARLIE BROWN

By VINCE GUARALDI

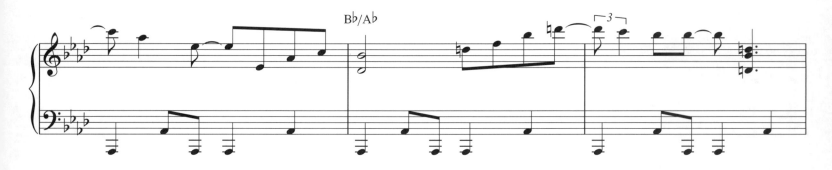

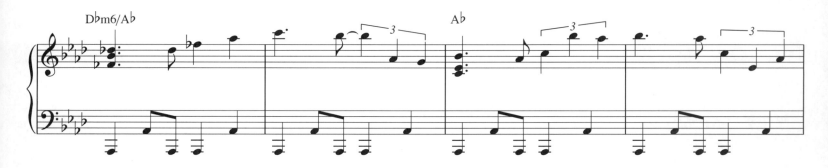

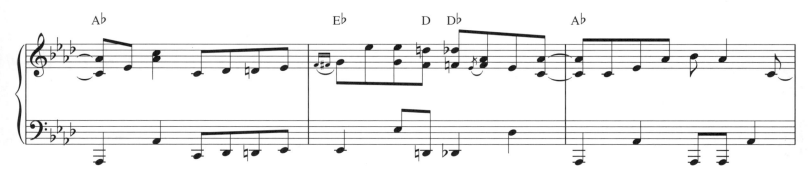

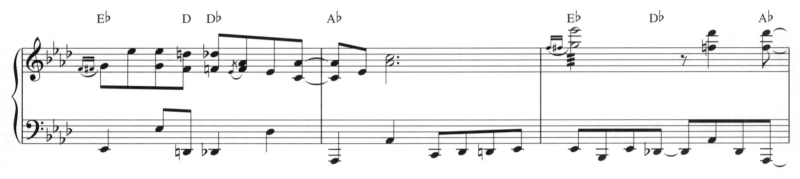

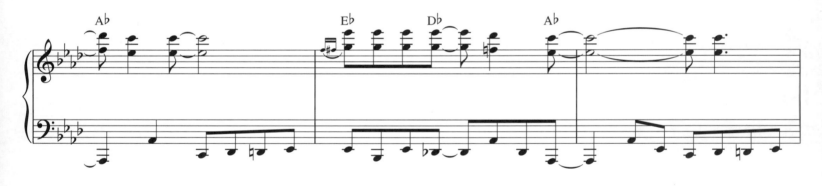

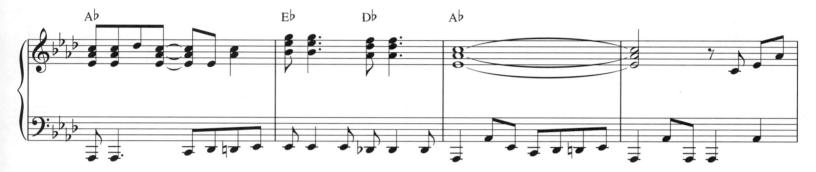

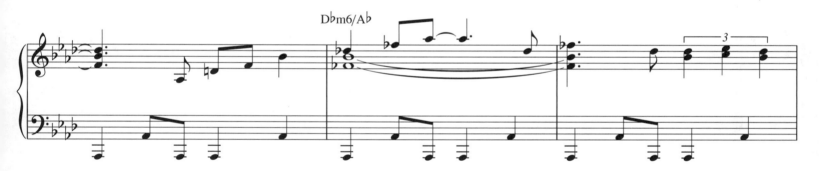

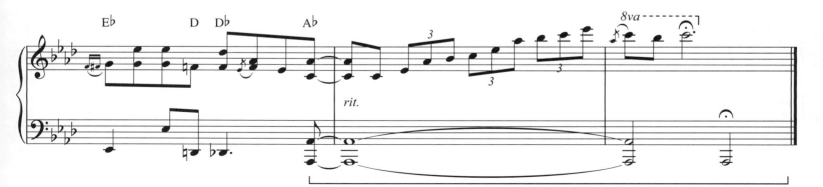

YOU'RE IN LOVE, CHARLIE BROWN

from YOU'RE IN LOVE, CHARLIE BROWN

Words by LEE MENDELSON
Music by VINCE GUARALDI

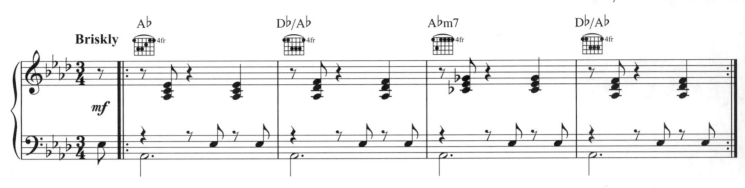

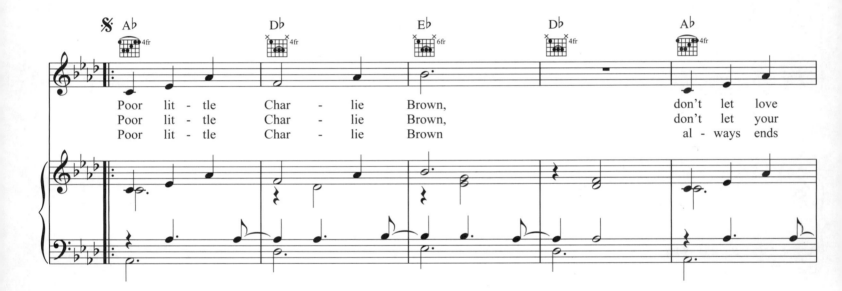

Poor lit - tle Char - lie Brown,   don't let love
Poor lit - tle Char - lie Brown,   don't let your
Poor lit - tle Char - lie Brown   al - ways ends

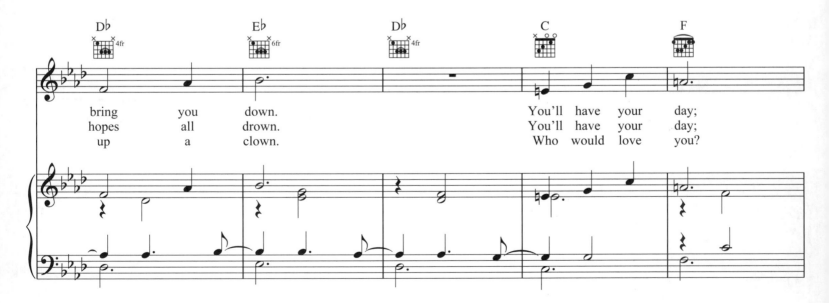

bring you down.   You'll have your day;
hopes all drown.   You'll have your day;
up a clown.   Who would love you?

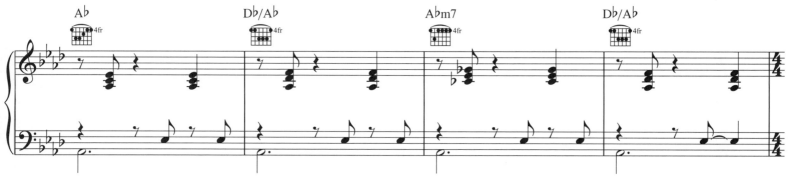

Moderately fast

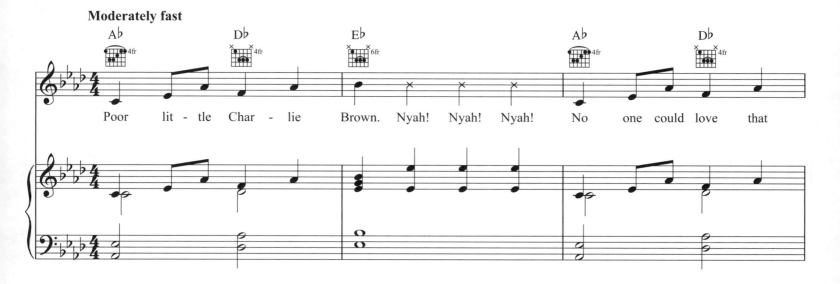

Poor lit-tle Char-lie Brown. Nyah! Nyah! Nyah! No one could love that

clown. Nyah! Nyah! Nyah! Who would love you? No one, that's who!

Your face is too darn round. Nyah! Nyah! Nyah! Your face is too darn round!

PLAY IT AGAIN, CHARLIE BROWN
from THERE'S NO TIME FOR LOVE, CHARLIE BROWN

By VINCE GUARALDI

Moderate Boogie Woogie

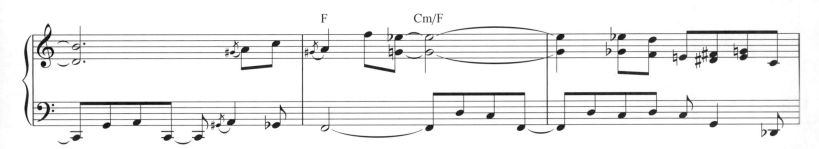

Solo section: two R.H. tracks arranged for an individual pianist.

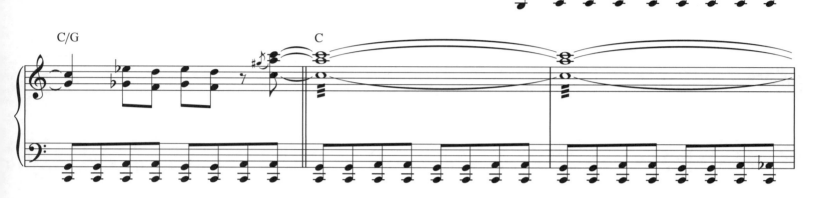

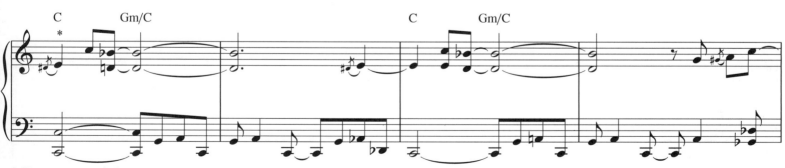

Piano as recorded

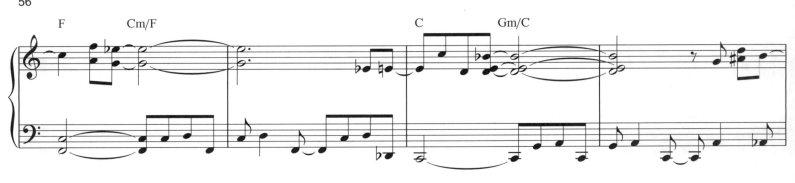

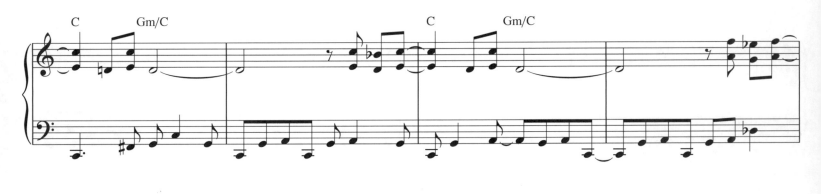

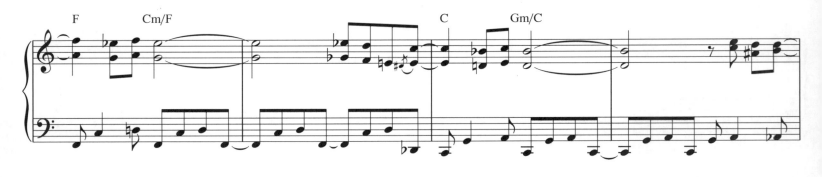

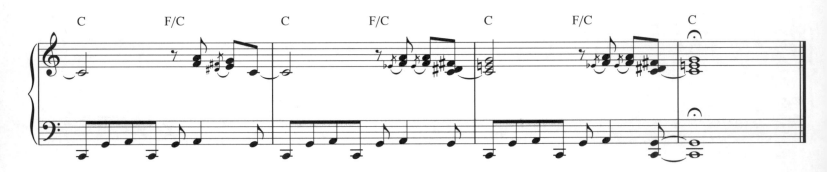